HOW BILLIONAIR BUSINESS LEADERS SOLVED
THE 8 MOST
CHALLANGING PROBLEMS
IN
MANUFACTURING AND PROJECT MANAGEMENT

(LEAN INTEGRATED DESIGN AND PRODUCTION)

1

CONTACT: +234 806 395 8922,
fullpowerprojects@yahoo.com

Content

CONTACT: +234 806 395 8922,
fullpowerprojects@yahoo.com

1

CHAPTER

**Overcoming Client's Negotiation
Impact on Production Plan**

1. PROBLEM

Clients often negotiate about the price
to the last moment, destroying the
possibility of orderly production
preparation; almost weekly are some
jobs rushed through the factory,
making it impossible to realize the
weekly production plan completely

CONTACT: +234 806 395 8922,
fullpowerprojects@yahoo.com

SOLUTION

HOW TO ORGANIZE PRODUCTION BETTER

For profit level to improve, the weekly production plan should be guided against client's negotiation techniques. Client's negotiation technique which is often about the price to the last moment has affected the possibility of orderly production preparation and in return does impacting on the weekly production plan.

It is so clear that the negotiation style chosen by the client is deliberate so to explore any possible profit. This is called "Delay Tactic". Delay tactic is advantageous to the client because it shifts the selling organization (Vendor) to a level of fear of not realizing there weekly target by so the client achieve a better price while the vendor is left with little or no time to deliver. Once the seller runs out of time, the seller is exposed to desperation. At that time they accept almost the price offered by the client in other to avoid total lost in that weekly production. For the supplier to maximise profit, is so obvious that various ways to tackle these prevailing issues from week in week out will be devised and these are from going back to the weekly plan, revisiting the critical path and treating it as a priority:

CONTACT: +234 806 395 8922, fullpowerprojects@yahoo.com

- Getting the negotiation team to be trained. That could be flexible in improving on negotiation strategies. Because it seems that clients negotiating teams are more experienced than the production organization team. Also, from the production weekly plan, a time should be scheduled for all the activities on the weekly production timeline. Starting from client's negotiation. And this time should be made known to the client from the beginning of negotiation. A well experienced negotiating team will work with the time scheduled for price negotiation and will employ the best tactic that will bring to play a win-win situation. Even at that, there should be little float added to negotiation activities for the worst case scenario.

- Placing a buffer between Clients negotiation and production preparation. It is optimum that production preparation is being given a priority by ensuring that negotiation is not delayed to shorten the duration allotted during the planning to production preparation. These shows that production preparation activity is on the critical path in the total production timeline. Starting from client's negotiation to concrete production and delivery. Going from observation over time. The preparation

5

time often don't have float so any delay from the negotiation impact on the production preparation and later evolve into affecting production proper. Resulting to rework often times. Concrete are rejected for not hitting the clients schedule and requirement because everything is done in a rush. It is so obvious that a working plan is required, that will eliminate the rush. In as much as cost is important (constraint) to every business it is not the only constraint that should be treated as priority. Part of the constraints is time also. In production organisation time is money. Strategy should be put in place to fight production out of lack of time. We loos quality, money and reputation when run out of time and do things in rush.

- Every team on the production line should have a buy-in to the weekly plan. A presentation should be conducted at the beginning of the week where which the final weekly plan will be acquainted to all functions in the line of production. Every team should be aware of when they come in and how long they are required to take in their activity.

- A war against rush and rework should be launched in the organisation. And

6

personnel should be trained to know how to avoid delay which is the root cause of rush that has made the organisation not to have gotten a maximised profit. Economically, when demand is high, supply also should be high for sellers to have a better profit at what they produce. But this principle has never been proven well in this case because of little supply of the highly demanded concrete. Yet in the organization the labour required to bring in a maximised profit are being hired. Finally, in this case I therefore recommend value of marginal product of labour where which every employee's input will account for the expended dollar.

CONTACT: +234 806 395 8922, fullpowerprojects@yahoo.com

2

CHAPTER

**Coordinating Design Changes
Without interrupting Workflow**

2. PROBLEM

**Drawings received are often
incomplete, and they keep changing,
which makes the preparation of
workshop drawings troublesome**

CONTACT: +234 806 395 8922,
fullpowerprojects@yahoo.com

SOLUTION

HOW TO ORGANIZE PRODUCTION BETTER

From participation and experience overtime in this organization, it is literally observed that Client's often don't know what they want. Which could be narrowed to the reason why the service of organization like this could be hired, so to help in the discovery and acquirement of what is needed by client. After that, clients need would become client's requirement to the performing organization. It is to the service providing vendor to meet client's requirement for the project to be successful. According to Huovila et al. (1994) one could easily missed requirement from various clients, if there is a poor management of their requirement. Most times clients come with unrealistic target, yet that could still be managed by letting them know the required quality is unrealistic with the available budget. It is worst when team member's inexperience to handle certain things count for part of what is setting the performing organization not to be able to match demand with supply.

In a project like this where various drawings are expected to be approved before finalising on the workshop drawings. There will be countless iterations going through stages to get buy-ins

9

and approval. Changes are bound to crop up in various ways and reasons but all these could not be possibly managed to a successfully end without notifying those responsible of the drawings about the plan and when they are expected to be through with all changes and input. There should be Design Structure Matrix (DSM) put in place in this organization. DSM is a tool built to help out with the simplification of the various interdependency between design activities and to coordinate the necessary iterations required to produce information according to Theoritical foundations: understanding the Basic concepts for Managing Production and Projects (Module 1: Learning package) by (Ricardo and Lauri 2014). This drawing problem could be resolved efficiently by representing inter relationship of drawing activities on matrix

Workshop drawing could not be completed if incomplete drawings are submitted. I am recommending training for the engineers that are responsible to feed in the initial drawings that will give rise to the workshop drawing. This training is to ensure that they understand that their deliverables are important to the success of the organisation. Secondly, they will be trained on how to understand each component of the required drawing and move on by getting it done before forwarding it to the next level.

10

CONTACT: +234 806 395 8922, fullpowerprojects@yahoo.com

For professional practise that this organization owes an obligation to comply and operate at, it is expedient a Change Control Board (CCB) is inaugurated to manage changes judiciously, because it seems that anybody can just stand and effect changes on drawings without observing lay down procedure for change management. These change control board is not that it will be acting like a murder Board by shooting down on team member's ideas that might lead to a breakthrough but rather it will serve as an authority to control changes. Changes could either be positive or negative; each should be evaluated and submitted to the CCB before effected on the working drawing if approved. Uncontrolled changes in drawing has often times reduce the morale and increase the frustration among those that are responsible of putting the final drawings together, Most times the CCB could have a policy that drawings among team should not be iterated more than three (3) times. Reasons for this, is to guide the scope against being impacted in various ways. Part of the CCB responsibility is to make known the timeline for various changes and when they could be welcome for deliberation. A Change Management Board CCB is not inaugurated to just track repository of changes. It is there to also encourage team members and stake holders on how worthwhile their ideas could be if innovative and how it could pioneer a better way of getting things done.

11

It is observed that drawings keep changing to what has been deliberated upon and rejected because there is no track of repository. All these would the CCB do if inaugurated. All proposed change passes through the Board either to be effected or rejected. Those effect and rejected have its descriptions and tracking number in the repository. With that it could be easily sported if that change was being re-proposed. These saves allot of time and effort, also protect scope against creeping on any side.

Production is a succeeding activity of the final drawing after all changes have been incorporated. Most times the project stay on and keep wasting time meant for other things in the drawing phase and at the end the final drawing is produce but there is not enough time for any other activity. If the above recommended are adopted in these organization, the issue of sending incomplete drawings that have made this organization to loos money will be fixed. Frustrations among the Engineers in charge of the final workshop drawing will be taking care of. Production will go smoothly without trying to gain time for activities.

CONTACT: +234 806 395 8922,
fullpowerprojects@yahoo.com

3

CHAPTER

**Maintaining the Schedule While
staying in front of the Team**

3. **PROBLEM**

   **Half of sites provide an orderly
   schedule for two weeks deliveries, but
   half hardly knows what they can
   install next week, however, they
   blame your company if they have
   nothing to install**

CONTACT: +234 806 395 8922,
fullpowerprojects@yahoo.com

SOLUTION

HOW TO ORGANIZE PRODUCTION BETTER

A typical of what this organization is passing through is what an organizations that folded up for not being able to generate profit that will keep them strong in the competition with its kind. There are specific things that have been ignored that have landed this organisation in this place where it has not been meeting up demand with supply. Something should be done and now is the time things should be done. Good a thing that management has identified the need for that and has gone ahead to ask for ideas that will turn things around. There are specific things that have been ignored which landed this organization at where it is today. Where which half of site could provide a two weeks working schedule for deliveries while the other half could barely know what is on the next timeline for them to install, so they go ahead blaming the company for not providing for them what to install. Is like that when specific things are not being observed, Part of which is the human resource is planning. This organization should have at list two weeks schedule for all staff ahead of time so this confusion can be fixed.

The Project Human Resource Plan comprises the various processes that organises, direct and manage the team. The production team will not

14

be complete without an assigned roles and responsibility for producing concrete down to the point of delivering it into the hands of the client and also ensuring that it is signed off by the client. Every one of the team member on the project must have a justified reason for staying on the production line even for a second. Why half of the production team knows what to do and has provided an orderly schedule for two weeks delivery and half of the site just loaf around blaming management without knowing what is expected of them to install next week is that team members are not included in the planning process. All team members and functions should have an input to the schedule development so there will be a buy-in. Team members should first incorporated in the decomposition of the Work Breakdown Structure (WBS) where which the schedule could be developed from.

Staffing Management Plan explains the actual time and the way resources (human) requirement can be fulfilled. And over time this will be updated. It will help spot out if actually there are nothing to install. Once there no activities for team members, they can then be relieved. The staffing Management Plan if being put in place will have a resource calendar. The resource calendar says exactly when the service of any personnel or function will be required. Its also will tell for how long will the service be required for each week or month. This are what could

15

help reduce the redundancies around the project site.

Responsibility Assignment Matrix (RAM): From the human resource plan it will be noted when each team member's service will be needed, what exactly the team member is coming to get done for the organization after being hired. And there is where we put the Responsibility Assignment Matrix (RAM) in place. It will connect all the work packages or activities to each personnel from the WBS.

Finally the communication link should be empowered. Where which we will redefine the reporting style of the project. The communication channels will be determined so to know how it ought to move around the site. All personnel will know who they are answerable to, what meeting they are meant to attend. So, things like the two weeks look-ahead schedule will be feasible to all function and department before hand. When communication plan is not a priority things like this happen around an organisation. The success of any organisation is how clear its communication plan could be to members. All plans, ranging from the sub plans to the production, delivery, whatever the plan could be should be clear to the least personnel in the organization

CONTACT: +234 806 395 8922, fullpowerprojects@yahoo.com

4

CHAPTER

**Keeping Track of Completed Modules
and still keep the factory/site
productive**

4. **PROBLEM**

**To keep the factory busy, the
production control policy is to have a
buffer of two weeks of completed
production (ready to be delivered),
however requiring two men to keep
track and sort out which modules are
where, and a large storage yard**

CONTACT: +234 806 395 8922,
fullpowerprojects@yahoo.com

SOLUTION

HOW TO ORGANIZE PRODUCTION BETTER

Part of what has made this organisation not to realise so much profit during this time that the market demand of our product is very high, is in the kind of policies and organizational rules that we have. There is need now to go through the root cause of the low turnout that has set this organisation not to be able to achieve its strategic goals for the past five years. Good rules bring about turn around to production and profit making. That is why first, we should concentrate on what we have done in the last few years that have landed us where we are today. Our movement is upward and forward, but the pace is not as anticipated. I would not out rightly want to say all our policies are not profit oriented, but some are, is just obvious that they are not the best for us. Our production-supply chain management is mostly the area I would want this organization to focus on improving in this year. Part of our policies that has not work so well for us in the product-supply chain management is the area where we had to keep the factory busy. The control policy there is the buffer of two weeks that we cascaded there in the production to delivery time line. Why would anyone want to keep the factory busy if it is not producing modules that are rightly needed? The

18

factory is for production and just-in-time delivery. We will have to reduce our waste by coping this overproduction that as encourage the buffer of two weeks for just sorting.

In this scenario what could be recommended is production realization for the arrangement of the management structure. According to Kagioglou et al.,(2007) in Theoritical foundations: understanding the Basic concepts for Managing Production and Projects (Module 1: Learning package) by (Ricardo and Lauri 2014) inception, conception, development and production could be made a collective whole. Design and production management is developing and could be taking as integral to product realization, and "design" could be referred as the contribution of all the "designers" that are part of production, ranging from architects, engineers, manufacturers to suppliers (Ricardo and Lauri 2014). It is true that products required to be sorted out after production so to have well organized packaging and delivery. I know it can also be credited because it has reduced the delivering of modules incomplete of accessories. Yet to make this better, a just in time delivery should be incorporated into the organization tradition, where which modules leaves the factory not more than twenty for hours after production. This suggested not to exceed twenty for hours is there to take care of packaging and final quality checks. We don't need much time for inspection since we have quality

CONTACT: +234 806 395 8922,
fullpowerprojects@yahoo.com

incorporated into the life cycle of the supply chain. To make these possible, modules to be produced should consider delivery strategy first before they are being sent in for production. There should be a delivery unit working with the inventory team and the production team. Modules are sorted out into production by the inventory team. This can take care of the need to want to sort things out after production. It cost this organisation allot of money, care and time to keep modules fallowing down in the storage unit for a second not to talk about two weeks. This keeps us spending money week in week out on security. Most times already produced modules ended up getting damaged in the storage yard because of the so many lifting and rearrangement during sorting and lead to wastage. Which we most times condemn and in the other cases we rework. It brings frustration to our personnel the way things come out of production on coordinated. In the production and delivery chain, sorting activity which would have not been in the critical path is now on it and we focus on it because of our challenging it has been. Until it is remove as execution activity and being made control activity it will always take this much stress. Referring to theoritical foundations: understanding the Basic concepts for Managing Production and Projects (Module 1: Learning package) production and product development of construction artefact, required an elaborate analyses on three angles, not only

20

on transformations, how activities flows and how value are generated (Tzortzopoulos, 2004).

For production to be controlled against waste as we so desire, the two men doing the two weeks sorting should be relief of their job after production and should be doing it before production or else their services will not be needed any longer because it has really not served the company any better. Here, we not just sharing ideas on how to organize production by relieving men, we are also going to be saving time, money reducing waste, which are the sole line lean production.

One key thing I have always wanted to do away with is the massive storage property yard that we have wasting in the name of sorting. We are not going to need that much if we fixed the sorting activities into inventory and production. What this organization looses weekly for maintenance of the storage yard alone, is massive and unimaginably not worthy for storing modules that have already been produced. We can actually generate money from all these in a short while and fixed in the expansion of our production unit, now especially that the market demand of our product is climbing so fast.

Part of what clients have recommended us for to others is our good quality. Quality is good because it send the costumer back smiling and comes back another day ready to pay more.

21

Credit to that, But we need to focus on something else and that is how some costumers are kept waiting for so long to get their modules delivered to them. Because of this, each week we record more than 70% of clients we could not get product for. This is because of our inability to produce more. Considering the above mentioned and inculcating them into how we work will bring a turn around.

CONTACT: +234 806 395 8922,
fullpowerprojects@yahoo.com

5

CHAPTER

The best Approach To Work in Progress Buffers in Work Station

5. **PROBLEM**

To keep each work station busy, there are work-in-progress buffers between them; however, sometimes these buffers grow to such sizes that it is a real wonder that anything can be kept moving

CONTACT: +234 806 395 8922,
fullpowerprojects@yahoo.com

SOLUTION

HOW TO ORGANIZE PRODUCTION BETTER

In recent time, production has grown to a fast pedestal and things like delay is no longer encouraging. Leading organization treat the timely delivery of product to the customer as priority. They continuously improve on strategies to facility the flow of activities among work station till the point of delivery. Work-in-progress buffers placed in between work stations are as result of overproduction. Overproduction is a waste of various kinds of industrial resources and that is what keeps the buffer growing to a level where which it is almost causing blockages to the flow of activities. As long as the flow of activities are restricted, costumers will be kept waiting. Costumers prefer a just-in-time delivery. Each day that produced modules are not delivered into the hands of the client, production has not ended. If products are not being delivered we owe the client and so we are losing money. It is more riskier to delay module in production than not have started the production. Waste of overproduction leads to waste of waiting.

However, to resolve this is to make exactly what is required. Production should be based on request. Production should not be a way ahead of schedule so over production will not be what is taking the whole man hour. Work-in-progress is just a manufacture way of giving excuses to clients whereas there is an incompetency manufacturer is trying to hide. Though, work in progress is natural but when is excessive is obvious that waste has occurred.

What could keep this organization competing with others is its effective use of time. Keeping costumers waiting is not a good way of doing business. Just-in-time delivery should be how we treat our customers by not producing what has not been requested by costumers. Request, design, production and delivery should be a complete whole, where which, we will start focusing on delivery from the point of request and include activities in the design and production phases that will enable delivery as soon as possible. There is no other ways to take bottleneck off among activities than to produce exactly what is needed and could be control, not even the lengthy time placed as buffer.

25

6

CHAPTER

Reducing Set-up Cost

6. PROBLEM

To reduce set up costs of moulds, similar modules from different orders are produced in the same batch

CONTACT: +234 806 395 8922, fullpowerprojects@yahoo.com

SOLUTION

HOW TO ORGANIZE PRODUCTION BETTER

Exactly, that which have made this organization not to have realized so much are the way we handle production. This is in the way the activities are being organized, from the point of customers request to production and delivery. Realizing profit is not only to get customer always ready at the door step of the organization paying for product but in the getting of what they requested and timely. Also, how the internal design, production and delivery activity is being coordinated to eliminate all kind of waste.

To reduce set up cost of moulds is a lean way of thinking, which is the future of construction as manufacturing. But lean does not encourage eliminating activity that brings little waste while retaining other activities that are causing a bigger waste in the process flow. Lean integrated design and production which is being proposed in this report encourages war against any form of wastage. Lean practitioners have come to a common ground of agreement that there are non-value adding wastes which are seven in number. These waste are called "The 7 waste Muda' " and this as explained by Bicheno

27

(1998). Set up waste falls under the categories of the seven wastes "Waste of waiting"

For this organization to flourish in profit, it will have to start looking at the three types of operations that would aid balance in any process along the production line, which could be used in cascading value into the value stream and the work flow. According to Monden (1992) these three are Value adding, essential non-value adding and Non-value adding. This three should be brought to a level in the process where which value adding activities could out way the other two. Any non value activity in the production line should be replaced with an activity that adds more value than what the other one was taking off the process.

The problem here is that this organization has not well understood the form of waste that could be associated to construction as manufacturing. And that will be outlined for everyone to know the varying level of industrial waste and the severity of each one of them to the goals and reputation of this organization. Considering reducing set-up cost alone is not sufficient in profit realisation. There should be a way of reducing the wastes that are associated with producing similar modules from different orders in same batch. That sounds nice but in practical is not helping because is time wasting along the line. The fact that customers would have to wait for others to come place demand of same kind

28

CONTACT: +234 806 395 8922,
fullpowerprojects@yahoo.com

before they could be sure of getting their deliverables, is away not a good way of doing business. Getting customers to wait is non-value adding activity that is severe (Critical) and also should be cut away from the organization production tradition. Product should be on first come basis. Not only that, it is vital we will be able to let clients know exactly when they will be getting what was requested at the point of request. Rather than waiting for other customers to come and place the order of same product before coming up with a date of delivery. It is not a standard professional practise that each time clients asked to know the actual date they would be getting their product at the point of request we say "we will get back to you on that, just place you request because that will help us in getting back to you" because we really on other request of same kind to go into the factory.. That is obscured, not in this 21st century production are done that way. We cutting away the waiting time which if is being plotted the waste of set-up could be more. Set up we can handle internally but having customer to wait is seriously fighting this organization backward from attaining its strategic goals.

CONTACT: +234 806 395 8922,
fullpowerprojects@yahoo.com

7

CHAPTER

Frequent Quality Issue: How to Keeping Defect Out of Your Process

7. **PROBLEM**

There are frequent quality problems, and actually there are two men going around sites to rectify the defects

CONTACT: +234 806 395 8922,
fullpowerprojects@yahoo.com

SOLUTION

HOW TO ORGANIZE PRODUCTION BETTER

Everything in manufacturing could be minimally accepted but not the waste of defect. Defect most times leads to rework which is what every leading production Organizations battles with both hands. It takes money time and quality reputation to get fix defect. When the customer's requirement is not being met, the Organization reputation bleeds. Defective component leads to substandard projects. Construction is termed not successful when there is defect. Weather buried among component or not. There are various anomalies in our quality culture that has lead to the continuous battling of correcting defect. Quality is supposed to be on a continuous improvement (Kaizen) not continues deterioration among production line. According to Bicheno (1998) Cost of Quality can be used as the principle to quantify the financial involvement in prevention and rectification of defect.

There should be prevention over inspection. Prevention keeps defects off the production processes, while Inspection keeps defects off the final Product so it will not get into the customer's hands. This encourages Quality control and quality assurance. For production to

31

CONTACT: +234 806 395 8922, fullpowerprojects@yahoo.com

stay defect free, quality must be assured and controlled because it has in it the practice of monitoring deliverables of carrying out quality activities to access behaviours and quickly come up with the required changes if there is anomaly, it also ensure continuous process improvement that would annihilate non-value added activities. (PMBOK 5TH EDITION). There should be deliberated quality activities to be performed all through the project lifecycle. Rather than having two men going round the site rectifying defect, the normal thinking issue that preventing defect has minimal cost than what is being spent on rectifying defect. Most times defects are uncovered during the inspection of these two men and later get into the customer's hands. Quality should be planned, designed and built-in rather than having it inspected. Quality management includes creating policies and procedures into all the activities that are associated with manufacturing of a customer required product. Ensuring that it meets the defined (agreed upon requirement) need of the project. Customer satisfaction is what being pursued so therefore defect should be kept out of the hands of the customer. The approach requires conformance to requirement. That which is said that the project will produce is what it must produce. There must be a fitness of use, therefore the product must satisfy real need.

To this a better quality plan is recommended, a quality plan the will treat quality from design down to delivery. The work should be performed correctly the first time because the cost of rework is an assassination of company's reputation. So this will have to be annihilated out of this organization way of doing business, is unhealthy. Quality requirement will be developed as part of the planning process. It will be considered from the planning stage on how quality will be measured and defect will be prevented.

Two men would not have to go round checking if produced modules are defective or not when quality is being built into the processes because there will be quality already in each activity among the processes. And the system will know quality as part of its way of behaving. The company can then do away with the waste of rework. This is like a zero defect policy, continuous improvement policy, war against rework and full empowerment of customer satisfaction. This is not new in the improvement of construction products only that this organization has ignored or probably have not get it right. The adoption of continuous improvement should be embraced fully with both arms. This practise is what is good for this organization. There is no almighty formula that will come and resolve the quality issues around but rather practicing the above mentioned as a culture. It is good to have quality department, but practicing it should be every ones responsibility. Everyone should be aware of the

33

requirement and contribute in the building of activities that will enable the organization to realise it with a fair cost.

Senior management has a role to play in quality actualization. They should provide the entire requirement that will encourage the dissemination of quality functions across the organization. Quality is not the responsibility of a certain department; it is rather everyone's duty to discharge dully across the lifecycle of the project.

CONTACT: +234 806 395 8922, fullpowerprojects@yahoo.com

8

CHAPTER

How to Retain Skilled People and Still Pay Workers per Module

8. PROBLEM

The workers get paid per module, which makes costing easier and provides a good incentive (it is thought), but anyway it is difficult to retain skilled people

SOLUTION

HOW TO ORGANIZE PRODUCTION BETTER

When workers are being paid per module the organization will find the costing more easily but that encourages several Essential non-value added activities that will eventually take the money being saved out of the coffer of the organization. Things like rush will be found in the system. Workers would be paying less attention at the quality of the module rather they will be focusing on their pay when the module is been signed off. It will be more difficult to retain skilled people because workers are not being treated as integral to the success of the organisation. Things that encourages skilled workers to stay with a particular organization is appraisals and being paid a premium or an incentives for attaining a milestone or finishing a successful project. People want to part of a system; they want to share in the successes and failures of an organization. The performing organization too will not be able chose the best workers that deserved to be retained from others.

The most important resources of any project are people, not just people but people with the required skills. So therefore retaining the best should be part of how we hire. There should be plan always running year-in year-out to retain the best found in any one of our project. This can only be made possible if workers are not paid per module. Anybody can talk about a successful project but a good Organisation will know that the best quality means the best skilled people around. The modules a created by people. So the best hands are to be kept. In as much as we want to make costing easier today, we should not derail from focusing on intellectual properties. People represent living brand. The sustainable intellectual property of this organisation is in constant reduction because people like this are leaving the organization. The recommended is to take the pain and do costing properly and stop paying workers per module because it is detrimental to the future of this organization. We can spot and retain the best if workers spend better time with us. And they will in return add value to the intellectual property of this organization.

We can talk about demand and the market of our supply. People with good understanding are needed to observe the trend and access the market of the behaviour and requirement of buyers and sellers and come up with value added strategy to get it fullfilled. There are various ways to motivate workers to want to stay with a particular organization, but that will be deliberately planned into the culture of the organization because workers will not be retained on automatic.

37

People are essential in the construction industry, a vital differentiator, and success, for an organization is how proficient it is in attracting, acquiring, developing, encouraging and retaining its most essential workforce. Actually the demand for skilled people is increasing. Companies are sourcing for specialized knowledge. It will have to be in our culture to never lack the skilled hands that will help deliver the best into the hands of our clients. Construction today is this competitive. We are here by encouraged to retaining the competency of always finding from in house the best around.

In the construction industry, skilled workers have the knowledge that they have a choice because there is always one company around sourcing for the best. They often favour the organization with well formidable ethical practice. They seldom go with name; rather they look also at the company records and tradition.

CONTACT: +234 806 395 8922,
fullpowerprojects@yahoo.com

REFERENCES

Bertelsen, S; and Koskela, L. J. (2002) Managing the three aspect of production in construction. In: Proceedings 10th annual conference of the International Group for lean Construction. Gramado, Brazil

Brookfield E; Emmitt, S; Hill, R and Skaysbrook, S. (2004). The architectural technologist's role in linking lean design with lean construction. In: Proceedings 10th annual conference of the International Group for lean Construction. Copenhagen, Denmark.

Bicheno, B (1998) The Quality 60: Aguide for Servicing and Manufacturing.

Huovila, P. (1994) Clients requirement Management.

Kagioglou, M; Tzortzopoulos, P; Fomoso, C and emmitt, S. (2007) product development and design management Retrieved from: http://www.iglc.net

Koskela, L. J. (2000) An exploration towards a production theory and its application to construction Technical Research Centre of Finland. Espoo, Helsinki university: 296

Monden, Y. (1992) Cost Management in the New Manufacturing Age: Innovation in the new Japanese Automotive industry.

Ricardo, C:, Owen, R. and Koskela, L J. (2014). Theoretical foundations: understanding the Basic concepts for Managing Production and Projects (Module 1: Learning package). Drawing Activity Matrix

Ricardo, C:, Owen, R. and Koskela, L J. (2014). Theoretical foundations: understanding the Basic concepts for Managing Production and Projects (Module 1: Learning package). Production and product development of construction artefact.

A Guide to The Project Management Bod y of Knowledge (PMBOK Guide) - Fifth Edition.

www.ingramcontent.com/pod-product-compliance
Lightning Source LLC
Chambersburg PA
CBHW070419190526
45169CB00003B/1335